EDUCATION THROUGH THE DECADES

EDUCATION THROUGH THE DECADES

AVERY NIGHTINGALE

CONTENTS

1 Introduction   1

2 Early 20th Century   3

3 Post-War Reforms   7

4 The 1960s and 1970s   9

5 Technological Advancements in Education   11

6 Education in the Digital Age   13

7 The Impact of Globalization   15

8 Current Challenges in Education   17

9 9   19

Copyright © 2024 by Avery Nightingale
All rights reserved. No part of this book may be reproduced in any manner
whatsoever without written permission except in the case of brief quota-
tions embodied in critical articles and reviews.
First Printing, 2024

CHAPTER 1

Introduction

Influence of a number of factors has been noted and might account for observed trends over the decades, including public interest, global economic status, availability of scholarships, interest in furthering special interests, and a draft (World War I, World War II, Vietnam). Nominally, other timeless factors such as institutional and program reputation as well as faculty and staff have been known to sway a scholar's decision. Another factor known to affect student preferences for certain majors is the availability of subsequent, desirable, and relevant careers, and more recently, the advent of globalization has created a need by technologically advanced nations for high-skilled, competitive workers in areas such as finance, technology, and the sciences.

Education is often hailed as a driving force behind advancements in various fields. Indeed, advances in modern medicine, technology, engineering, and the sciences often stem from a broad foundational knowledge base and from continuing education beyond initial degrees. Since its establishment in 1863, October, the Massachusetts Institute of Technology (MIT) has aimed to produce—and to serve as a laboratory for the production of—frank and earnest men (and later, women). Six years into the study on undergraduate Enrollment and Degrees in the Sciences, the 20th century saw several major scientific breakthroughs, the first cars for personal use, the Wright brothers' pioneering flights, and global war, often taking research and development in areas such as weaponry and medicine to unprecedented levels (only aeronautic advances enabled the moon landing in 1969).

CHAPTER 2

Early 20th Century

Because of this practical ideology, teachers were taught strictly that the first emphasis of education would be upon the acquisition of life skills. As society continued to modernize, there was a shift away from skilled work that could be done at home to industrial work. Former President John Quincy Adams observed that even as early as 1825 there was growing concern about industrial education and how the railway locomotive "is employed to spin mills, to forge iron, and to perform an endless succession of mechanical operations." This new wave of technology eliminated the vocational need for skilled individuals who could make a product from start to finish. As a result, the number of manual workers increased significantly in the United States between 1890 and 1920. Population Economics: At the time when these societal changes were taking place, children in the lower and middle-class homes had no option in the type of employment that was available to them.

In the early 20th century, the purpose of education at all levels was to develop productive workers with practical skills, instead of preparing them for the college degree programs that would give them a broader understanding of the world. In 1900, only 10-15% of public high school-age students were actually attending high school and when they did, the students were not exposed to a well-rounded curriculum or practical one. Teachers in elementary and secondary education taught students basic skills like reading, writing, and math. According to an article, the argument in support of trained labor forces "was based on industrial policy grounds, not on altruistic concerns about job opportunities or on taxpayer or consumer objectives".

WORLD WAR II ERA

Society and the world of education underwent many changes during this time, affecting people across the United States. In Kansas, in 1941, the legislature changed the name of "Industrial Education" to "Industrial Arts." All federal programs came under the Comprehensive Vocational Education Act of 1963, with Title IV being the Vocational Education Act of 1963. Federal funding began to support secondary schools for the development of Local Area Vocational Education School Programs, which included secondary vocational schools. This legislation allowed schools to update their curricula and acquire new equipment. Federal funds started reaching Kansas educators in 1964, with the Kansas Legislature supporting the act by providing forty-five percent of the implementation cost.

In Kansas, the value of diverse educational experiences was recognized in the Kansas Vocational Curriculum Guide–197. By the end of World War II, significant changes had occurred in education, impacting all aspects of it.

The World War II era (1941-1946) was a time of great change and challenges for the nation. Despite being at war, civilian life continued. In May 1942, the Menninger Clinic in Topeka and the U.S. Surgeon General's Office sponsored a national conference on Mental Hygiene in School Health. The first section of this document, handed down to school authorities, stressed the importance of preparing the new generation for post-war life. It emphasized the need for them to have a greater capacity for constructive living and problem-solving than any previous generation.

CHAPTER 3

Post-War Reforms

Post-World War I America, one of the most successful results of this self-education was the adaptation of the "adjustment" curriculum, which typified the schools of that era. This was particularly true in schools associated with social, economic, and/or geographic factors. Approximately 60% of white youth of high school age were in school, and the completion rate was between 33 and 35%. Caroline Haslett lays the responsibility for the woman's failure to progress to the successful completion of the goals laid out by her early educational undertakings. Edward V. Anderson and Elizabeth E. Nelson state in the Outlook of Education that the normal educational progress of women in general was hampered by "inherited home duties with 3 out of 4 daughters leaving home immediately after graduation."

Also known as traditional schooling, the grammar schools of this era were modeled after those in England, teaching the basics of reading, writing, and arithmetic, as well as religion and manners. Classroom sizes remained small, which enabled a high level of individual instruction. Teaching, in most parts of the country, was done by men and women outsiders to the community. Attendance was based upon the ability to pay, for males because of the cost of room and board, and for females through the lack of schools in the vicinity and the demands of household duties.

CHAPTER 4

The 1960s and 1970s

The University of Colombo and two of its affiliated colleges, the science faculty of the University of Peradeniya and Sri Jayawardenapura University at Gangodawila, Nugegoda, continued to work in association with their counterparts in London in relation to the EASLEP (English as a second language examination for Proficiency). The EASLEP introduced the continuous system of evaluation for students, and their standards were noted in the certificates as permanent records. In terms of language proficiency, at that time (during the early 1970s), the 'passage level' was in between that of the final level of ALL (Advanced level language) and the EASLEP (GCE) O/L standard. SPILMUN5 was successfully conducted on lines of the UN General Assembly conference thereafter.

There was much less funding for interest in education from the government during the 1970s. The government had shifted towards the view that employment was more important for students than education is. In this sense, they seemed to place higher emphasis on industries and trade. It was a difficult stage for all educators, including language educators. The efforts made by the pioneers of language teaching to teach the English language to their students were beginning to produce results during this period. There were also many talented language teachers who emerged from the schools. Despite the lack of resources, these teachers were able to motivate their students to learn. Although all those who studied English were not able to go beyond the ordinary level, participation in SLEP (second language English proficiency) test gradually increased, and many who took part were able to secure high grades.

CHAPTER 5

Technological Advancements in Education

Efforts during the decade of the 2010s to integrate technology into the educational process included personalized web-based learning environments, games enabled with augmented reality technology, applications that support adaptive learning technologies, and interactive online textbooks. Literacy training for children who were growing up as digital natives (or in an environment that embraced multimedia and interactive media technologies) is another area that has been explored and found to be successfully achieved using technology. Dissatisfaction with the old systems, accompanied by an ambitious focus on improving 21st-century skills such as the abilities to guide and engage in collaborative and cooperative teamwork, effectively solve complex problems individually and collectively, and objective-driven technological skills and competencies for the purpose of pursuing higher education, careers, or for discreet technological integrations in content and national standards, represent some degree of pressure for many national educational systems worldwide.

Educators accept that technology is considered so beneficial to the advancement of students' careers and livelihoods that access to technology, such as computers and the internet, has been labeled by the FCC as a prerequisite for achieving successful education. In the meantime, some educators fear that the widespread use and integration of technology could detract from conventional methods of education. A commonly held point of view maintains that the endeavor to move from the traditional factory-based model of mass education to a learner-focused model facilitated by technology in the 21st century could take a minimum of 50 years.

CHAPTER 6

Education in the Digital Age

A re there any other threats for modern education in the digital information space? If we talk about secular education in Russia, of course, there are such threats. Certainly, contemporary digital communications offer advantages only to those who are quick-witted, spontaneous, interested in a wide variety of facts and facts about events happening in the world, i.e. to those who have average and wider information literacy, besides technical culture.

Besides, the most important factor, in my opinion, of the specific age-related opportunities of digital devices for studying and development of the younger generation is their ability to accelerate the rate and the depth of the cognitive and practical activities and to simplify, sometimes extremely, the performance arrangements of any, including most complex creative and searching tasks. What I have in mind here are: network databases, professional software, useful mobile applications.

And finally, we must come to the last decade in which trends in education have emerged and developed. One cannot but note an unequivocal "technologization" of education. Elements of interactive lessons, given through both computer programs and using the interactive whiteboard, are already moving from "a luxury" into common practice. With the click of a mouse, an elementary school student in a small town of Kaluga or a boy from a distant province of Kalmykia can attend a virtual tour of the British Royal Residences – and such lessons, incidentally, are becoming a quite common practice. Of course, the electronic mass media, including the Internet, television, radio, and other digital tools, are used not only in the interests of intellectual enlightenment of the pupils – movies, popular music, and computer games serve for that purpose as well among the others – though they are capable of really broadening the students' horizons and general educational panorama.

CHAPTER 7

The Impact of Globalization

The increasing international mobility of educational professionals has transformed tertiary education institutions into melting pots. As a result, an especially dynamic sector, higher education has become a facilitator (enhancer) of economic, social, and cultural globalization. Higher education institutions are likely to provide a pool of professional knowledge workers and to contribute to the creation of an 'international intelligent' labor force. While these are among the real benefits underpinning the drive for better and wider access to higher education, commercial and political interests continue to be the driving forces behind institutional and national/international Europeanization issues.

Another significant aspect of globalization is the increasing international mobility of students, teachers, professors, and other educational professionals. The mobility of studying is one of the primary concerns of internationalization. Unlike other service markets, the international transfer of 'consumers' appears to be a unique feature of tertiary education. The latest Institute of International Education (IIE, 2009) report estimated the number of internationally mobile students to be around 3.3 million in 2008. According to OECD data, half of these internationally mobile students are hosted by the United States, the United Kingdom, Australia, and Germany. As tertiary education systems are globalizing, there are clear winners and losers in the competition for international students.

CHAPTER 8

Current Challenges in Education

Diversification of students' interests has resulted in a lack of seriousness in the academic activities amongst them. Further, the students are more captivated by the sports and literary activities at the expense of their studies, and they are not well aware of the curriculum of their subjects. This sort of disinterest amongst the youth ranging from 17 to 19 years of age at the completion of their higher secondary education is the problem that we are confronted with. Lack of seriousness emanating from diverse interests augmented drop in learning achievements on the part of the secondary students. It is a stark reality that the learning achievements amongst the high students are not at all encouraging. A well-thought strategy is needed to give and inculcate seriousness in the youth so that they can be aware and conscious of the realities of their curriculum as well as the extent to which they have been able to bridge the gap in their learning.

In 1945, a report titled "Higher Education for American Democracy" was published. It sought, among other things, for higher education to promote a robust, free, and democratic society. The report posited that the purpose of education was twofold: first, it was to expect the individual and country's social and economic development; and second, it was to contribute to democracy, world peace, and better living standards of people. When Mahatma Gandhi took up the National Education assignment in the 1930s, he had very clear ideas of the direction that Indian education must take. "I would live the life in accordance with principles of goods such as truth or non-violence and minimize suffering from all others in my immediate environment. And I shall endeavor to train others also to live as I have been trying to live."

CONCLUSION

Societal values at the time will always place pressure and irrevocably place ubiquitously unseen limitations on the ways in which education is reformed. Learning is an insight into performance, ability, and perspective. The values and rationales with which a society operates will always reflect hypotheses about human learning. Futurists will continue to reflect, model, and make troubling predictions about the future, but to evoke a phrase once more, it is – and always will be – the learners who have the final say. In the future, there will still be learners. There will be personalities, possibly with genes. There will be environments – whether arbitrary or planned. There will be education. When all is said and done, it is education that empowers the learner; empowering learners becomes the proclaimed raison d'être.

It would be easy to suggest that the future for education is bleak. Many are now losing their faith in the domestic and global economy. Public sector actions are an ongoing concern, as cuts are extended and head teachers are 'given' the opportunity to take control of more of their schools' services. Compounding the issue of a possible failure of support from public sector departments is governmental policy, which is currently being set and appears to contain some reforms that go against the support schools are being offered, mostly from the relatively new Coalition government. Evidence would suggest that we are losing our societal value of education. Vision and values may be developed for schools and the children they are privileged to teach; however, these are seldom enacted upon in the non-educational world. It is an atmosphere of such that requires a positive outlook at this moment in time, and it is our role to be future generations of learners to provide others with alternative directions and visions: Leading the learners and the learning; empowering the learner and learning. With education, it is always the learners who are the main reason, the beginning, and the end.

www.ingramcontent.com/pod-product-compliance
Lightning Source LLC
Chambersburg PA
CBHW051411130726
47987CB00007B/2944